ON THE WAY HOME

"*LITTLE HOUSE*" Books by Laura Ingalls Wilder

Laura and Almanzo shortly after their marriage in De Smet, Dakota Territory.

ON THE WAY HOME

THE DIARY OF A TRIP FROM SOUTH DAKOTA

TO MANSFIELD, MISSOURI, IN 1894

by LAURA INGALLS WILDER

with a setting by Rose Wilder Lane

HARPER & ROW, PUBLISHERS, NEW YORK AND EVANSTON

LIST OF ILLUSTRATIONS
with captions by Rose Wilder Lane

ON THE WAY HOME

I

For seven years there had been too little rain. The prairies were dust. Day after day, summer after summer, the scorching winds blew the dust and the sun was brassy in a yellow sky. Crop after crop failed. Again and again the barren land must be mortgaged, for taxes and food and next year's seed. The agony of hope ended when there was no harvest and no more credit, no money to pay interest and taxes; the banker took the land. Then the bank failed.

In the seventh year a mysterious catastrophe was world-wide. All banks failed. From coast to coast the factories shut down, and business ceased. This was a Panic.

It was not a depression. The year was 1893, when no one had heard of depressions. Everyone knew about Panics; there had been Panics in 1797, 1820, 1835, 1857, 1873. A Panic was nothing new to Grandpa, he had seen them before; this one was no worse than usual, he said, and nothing like as bad as the wartime. Now we were all safe in our beds, nobody was rampaging but Coxey's armies.

All the way from California Coxey's Armies of Un-employed were seizing the railroad trains, jam-packing the cars and running them full speed, open throttle, hell-for-leather toward Washington. They came roaring into the towns, yelling "Justice for the Working Man!" and stopped and swarmed out, demanding plenty to eat and three days' rations to take with them, or they'd burn the town. People gave them everything to get rid of them. In all the cities Federal troops were guarding the Government's buildings.

I was seven years old and in the Second Reader at school but I had read the Third Reader and the Fourth, and Robin-son Crusoe and Gulliver's Travels. The Chicago Inter-Ocean came every week and after the grown-ups had read it, I did. I did not understand all of it, but I read it.

It said that east of the Miss-Issippi there were no trains on the railroad tracks. The dis-patchers had dis-patched every train to the far-away East to keep them safe from Coxey's Armies. So now the Armies were dis-banded and walking on foot toward Washington, robbing and raiding and stealing and begging for food as they went.

For a long time I had been living with Grandpa and Grandma and the aunts in De Smet because nobody knew what would become of my father and mother. Only God knew. They had diff-theer-eeah; a hard word and dreadful. I did not know what it was exactly, only that it was big and black and it meant that I might never see my father and mother again.

Then my father, man-like, would not listen to reason and

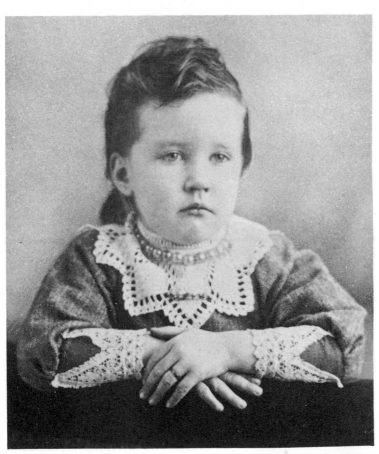

I was 2 years 4 months old when this picture was taken in April, 1889. I remember the picture-taking well, was impressed by the photographer's stupid pretense that there was a little bird in the camera. The photographer also kept putting my right hand on top of the left, and I kept changing them back because I wanted my carnelian ring to show. And in the end I won out.

stay in bed. Grandma almost scolded about that, to the aunts. Bound and determined to get out and take care of the stock, he was. And for working too hard too soon, he was "stricken." Now he would be bed-ridden all his days, and what would Laura do? With me on her hands, besides.

But when I saw my father again he was walking, slowly. He limped through the rest of his ninety years and was never as strong as he had been.

We lived then in our own house in De Smet, away from Main Street, where only a footpath went through the short brown grasses. It was a big rented house and empty. Upstairs and down it was dark and full of stealthy little sounds at night, but then the lamp was lighted in the kitchen, where we lived. Our cookstove and table and chairs were there; the bed was in an empty room and at bedtime my trundle bed was brought into the warmth from the cookstove. We were camping, my mother said; wasn't it fun? I knew she wanted me to say yes, so I did. To me, everything was simply what it was.

I was going to school while my father and mother worked. Reading, writing, spelling, arithmetic, penmanship filled days almost unbearably happy with achievements satisfying Miss Barrows's strict standards. "Procrastination is the thief of time," I wrote twenty times in my penmanship book, without error or blot; and "Evil communications corrupt good manners," and "Sweet are the uses of adversity," every t and d exactly twice as tall as a vowel and every l exactly three times as tall; every t crossed; every i dotted.

4

Almanzo at the time of THESE HAPPY GOLDEN YEARS.

All the way home down the long board walk in late afternoons we diligent scholars warmly remembered our adored Miss Barrows's grave, "Well done," and often we sang a rollicking song. It was the song of those days, heard more often than Ta-ra-ra boom-de-ay. My aunt Grace, a jolly big girl, often sang it, sometimes my mother did, and nearly all the time you could hear some man or boy whistling it.

> O Dakota land, sweet Dakota land,
> As on thy burning soil I stand
> And look away across the plains
> I wonder why it never rains,
> Till Gabriel blows his trumpet sound
> And says the rain has gone around.
> We don't live here, we only stay
> 'Cause we're too poor to get away.

My mother did not have to go out to work; she was married, my father was the provider. He got a day's work here and there; he could drive a team, he could carpenter, or paint, or spell a storekeeper at dinner-time, and once he was on a jury, downtown. My mother and I slept at Grandma's then, every night; the jury was kept under lock and key and my father could not come home. But he got his keep and two dollars every day for five straight weeks and he brought back all that money.

My mother worked to save. She sewed at the dressmaker's from six o'clock to six o'clock every day but Sunday and then came home to get supper. I had peeled the potatoes thin and set the table. I was not allowed to touch the stove. One

Laura at the time of THESE HAPPY GOLDEN YEARS.

day my mother made sixty good firm buttonholes in one hour, sixty minutes; nobody else could work so well, so fast. And every day, six days a week, she earned a dollar.

We were going to The Land of the Big Red Apple when we had enough money. Someone named Mr. Sherwin had gone there and seen it, so the pictures that he sent back were true; pictures of huge red apples and of rows of much smaller trees, and of buildings confusingly named Mansfield. They were not a man's field, and the print under them said they were The Gem City of the Ozarks.

Around and under these pictures on beautifully shiny paper I read that The Gem City of the Ozarks was in The Land of the Big Red Apple in Missouri. Now I knew three Miss States: Miss-issippi, Miss-consin, and Miss-ouri. Paul said, scornfully, that it wasn't Miss-consin, it was *Wis*-consin, but Wis didn't make sense to me.

Paul and George Cooley were coming with us to The Land of the Big Red Apple. Paul was oldest, George was next, I was only the youngstest but they had to let me boss because I was a girl. We had always known each other. Their father had two big teams and two big covered wagons, and Paul would be allowed to drive one of them; he said his father said he could. I did not want to believe this but I knew that Paul would never lie. He was a big boy, too, going on ten years old.

My mother had saved one hundred dollars to take to The Land of the Big Red Apple. All those dollars were one piece of paper, named "a hundred dollar bill." She hid it in

A sewing box made of cigar boxes by Almanzo for a first anniversary gift to Laura. It came with us in the hack to Mansfield.

her writing desk, a fascinating wooden box which my father had made and polished so shiny-smooth that stroking it was rapture. It opened on little brass hinges to lie spread flat and be a slanting green felt surface to write on. At the top was a darling wooden tray to hold my mother's pearl-handled pen, and beside this was an ink-well. And the green felt was on a lid that lifted up on tinier hinges to reveal the place for writing paper, underneath it. I was allowed to see and touch the desk only when my mother opened it.

The hundred dollar bill was a secret. My mother locked it in the desk. Mr. and Mrs. Cooley knew, perhaps Paul and George did, but we must not talk about it. I must never, never, speak one word about that hundred dollar bill, not to anyone. Never, no matter what happened.

In the shade of the big empty house my father painted our covered wagon. It was really better than a covered wagon; it had been a two-seated hack though now it had only the front seat. My father painted it shiny black. He made a flat top for it, of black oilcloth, and put straight curtains of the black oilcloth on both sides and the back. Each curtain would roll up when he pulled a rope. Behind the seat he fitted the bedsprings and my mother made up the bed on them. At night she would make my bed on the floor in front of the seat.

She baked two dozen hardtacks for the journey. They were as large as a plate, flat and hard. Being so hard and dry, they would not spoil as bread would. It was a hard tack to gnaw, but it tasted almost like a cracker.

We were going to make haste, driving every day to reach The Land of the Big Red Apple and get settled before winter. We could not stop to look for work, but we would need more food on the way, so my father bought a box of asbestos fire-mats to trade, or to sell for ten cents apiece.

Fire-mats were a new thing, unheard-of. They looked like round pieces of gray-white pasteboard edged with a narrow strip of tin. Nobody could believe that they would not burn, till my father proved it. He would urge doubters to make a hot fire, hotter and hotter, then he laid one of those mats right into the flames. It would glow red and the watchers would jeer, but that mat came out unharmed. Put one of those fire-mats under a pot, my father would say, and the pot could boil bone-dry, not a potato in it would so much as scorch. Every woman alive needed one of those mats.

Everything that we were taking all the way was packed under the bedsprings first. Next, the things that we would be using: the table and chairs with folding legs and the sheet-iron campstove that my father had made; the hammock that blind Aunt Mary had netted and given to us as a parting present; the writing desk, well wrapped; plates, cups, frying pan, coffee pot, wash basin, water pail, picket ropes and pegs; the hardtack in its box. My father tied down the back curtain. Outside it he fastened the hencoop while the hens fluttered and squawked inside the wire netting. But they would soon be used to traveling.

In the dawn next morning we said goodby to Grandpa

and Grandma, to the aunts Mary and Carrie and Grace, who all stood around to watch us go, though Aunt Mary's beautiful blue eyes could not see us. The mares were hitched to the hack; their colts, Little Pet and Prince, would follow them. The Cooleys' covered wagons had gone ahead, and Paul was driving the second one. I climbed up over our wagon's wheel and onto the seat by myself. My mother sat beside me; beside her my father tightened the lines; everyone said, "Goodby, goodby!" "Don't forget to write. I won't, I will, you be sure to. Goodby!" and we drove away.

Away from Grandma's house with its rag-carpets and rocking-chair, the hymn books on the organ, my very own footstool; away from the chalky schoolroom where angelic Miss Barrows taught Kindergarten, Primer, First and Second Readers; away from the summer sidewalks where grasshoppers hopped in the dry grass and the silver-lined poplar leaves rattled overhead; away from the gaunt gray empty house, and from Mrs. Sherwood and her sister who sometimes on sweltering afternoons asked me to fetch ten cents' worth of icecream from the far-away icecream parlor, and shared it with me; away from De Smet to The Land of the Big Red Apple.

My mother made daily notes of our journey in a little 5-cent Memorandum book, writing with pencil on both sides of the pages, of course. Nobody then wasted paper. This is her record.   R.W.L.

Pa and Ma Ingalls' house in De Smet. This picture was sent to us in Mansfield some years after we left Dakota.

Calumet Avenue, De Smet, South Dakota, around 1900.

II

July 17, 1894

Started at 8:40. Three miles out, Russian thistles. Harvesters in poor wheat. Crossed the line into Miner County at 2 o'clock. Camped by a spring that cannot be pumped, but there is feed for the horses. Grain about 8 inches high, will go about 1 ½ bushels to the acre. Hot wind.

July 18

Farmers mowing the grain for hay. At 11:30 we left Howard one mile east. Farm work well along here. Dragging for next year's crop is all done, without troubling to take this year's grain off. Worst crops we have seen yet. No grass. Standing grain 3 inches high, burned brown and dead.

Crossed the Northwestern R.R. tracks at 2:25. Crossed the line into McCook County at 5 o'clock, drove 2 ½ miles and camped. We had a little dust storm in the afternoon and drew the wagons up close together for we could not see what was coming. The wind changed from a hot south wind to a cold north wind, both *hard*. Though the thermometer stood at 102° in the wagon.

July 19

It rained in the night but did not blow. Nothing in the wagons got wet except one horse blanket. We had fried chicken for breakfast and got a late start at 9:15. Weather is cool and pleasant, wind in the north and dust laid by the rain. Groves are thick and look so nice but farmers are mowing their grain for hay.

We found a good camping place down in a ravine, out of the wind and nearly out of sight. Cooked our supper and ate it. As we were washing the dishes a man came and said if the man that owned the place saw us he would make us trouble, and as he lived just over the hill we thought we would move across the road and be all right there. So we hitched up and drove across. It was a very nice camping place. In the evening two men came up to talk. The thermometer stood at 92°.

Mrs. Cooley and I went to a house to buy milk. It was swarming with children and pigs; they looked a good deal alike.

July 20

Started at 1:10. One of the Cooleys' horses cut his leg a little in a barb wire fence.

We left Bridgewater half a mile to the east. Mr. Cooley drove into the town but we went on just south of it with the rest of the teams, and we came to the first piece of oats worth cutting that we have seen since we left De Smet, and they are not very good.

We watered the teams at a public well with windmill, by the side of the road. The water is good all through McCook County. Wells are 120 feet deep on the average and nearly every well has a windmill. This is a good county. All through McCook, this year is the first crop failure in 16 years. There are lots of groves of trees, and nice houses, big corncribs, many hogs; but we have not seen many cattle though there is a creamery in Bridgewater. The people say the corn crop is very poor but it is the best we have ever seen at this time of year.

Crossed the line into Hutchinson County at 10. Here they are mowing buffalo grass for hay. We passed a great pile of stones that had been cleared off the land. Saw some good wheat. Mr. Cooley overtook us at 12 o'clock when we came to a Russian settlement. He had not been able to get grain or any feed in Bridgewater though there are three mills in the town.

The Russian settlement—adobe houses, barns and chicken houses, and piles of peat to burn. The houses are back from the road and most of them are built long, the house in one end and the barn in the other. We stopped at one house for water. There was an idiot there, a full grown man, an awful sight.

We can see timber along the Jim River. It is only six miles away on our right hand, but 18 miles ahead of us. This is nice country but as one Russian said, "Nix good this year, nix good last year." We carried water in the wagons and camped without water, in a very good place except for that lack. Thermometer at 100° in the wagon.

The road has been almost perfectly level for two

days, only now and then a small ravine, no hills. Land here is priced from $2,500. to $3,000. a quarter section. [160 acres.]

July 21

Thought we would get an early start but everything went wrong, of course. We are out of bread so baked biscuit, and we made gravy with the chicken we cooked last night, poured it over the biscuits and called it chicken pie. When we were hitching up we let go of old Pet and she started off. Manly* had the halter off Little Pet so she could not go after her mother. I said Whoa and went toward her and as soon as she saw I was coming she ran. I could not catch her. Mr. Cooley chased her on his pony and they were far away before he could head her. She was going to Missouri without waiting for us. We finally got started at 8:20.

We are going gradually down toward the river. It is only 5 miles south west of us and there is timber thick along its bank. Harvesting and stacking is done here, and plowing begun.

At 10:30 the bluffs across the Jim river are in sight.

At 12 we crossed the line into Yankton County and

* Almanzo Wilder.

now at 2:15 we are on the Jim river flats. And they are flat as a floor. Some grain fields are on them, and meadows, and beside the road are two natural-grown trees, the first we have seen, and little scrubs they are, too.

160 acres of corn are in sight on one side of the road, and 80 on the other, at 4 P.M.

We have camped on the James river, down among the trees by a water mill. It is a very pleasant place. Only we are not far from a family or settlement of Russians. They all seem to be one family but Manly said he counted 36 children all the same size and Mr. Cooley says there are 50 all under 15 years old. They come down to our camp and stand around and stare at us.

The man who seems to be the head of the tribe, or commune or whatever it is, said they came here five years ago and now they own 17 quarter sections. They have herds of cattle, good horses, and 300 geese.

Just at dusk a boy came with a great big fish and wanted to know if we would pay for it. The men were gone and Emma Cooley and I did not know what it was worth. The boy said we might have it for a dime but Emma and I could not scrape up a dime between us.

We were about to give up, when the men came and bought the fish. In a few minutes the boy came back with two smaller ones and wanted 15 cents for them but finally took ten.

We are going to sleep tonight to the sound of running water. Manly killed a snake this eve.

Sunday, July 22

We all took a bath this morning. Mr. and Mrs. Cooley and the children went into the river. Paul and George had a rope around them and tried to swim. Rose went out with Mrs. Cooley, she had a rope around her and I held onto its end. She went out waist deep and paddled around, and sat down up to her chin.

The Russians have hung around us all day, children and grown folks both. They cannot talk and they understand only a little. They are very kind, they brought milk and a great pan of biscuits, and gave them to us, showing us that they were presents. The biscuits are light and very good. We got to feel a little acquainted with the folks, told them all our names and asked theirs and let them swing in the hammock and sit in the chairs. They are very curious and want to examine everything, talking about it to each other.

They wanted us to come to their houses, so Manly and I went. They showed us the geese and we watched the milkmaids milk. They look like the pictures of German and Russian milkmaids and peasants. Their yellow hair is combed smooth down each side of their faces and hangs in long braids behind and they wear handkerchiefs over their heads. They are all dressed alike. There are no sleeves in the women's long blue calico dresses but under them they wear white shirts with long white sleeves. The men have whiskered cheeks and long golden beards. They wear blue blouses that hang down long, to their knees almost, with belts around their waists. They were all very polite and smiling, seeming to try to say they were glad we came. They gave us another big pail of the fresh warm milk and Manly gave them a fire mat. One man seemed quite Americanized, Manly said to him slowly that the mat will not burn and he said that he understood. He may not believe it but if he tries it he will find out.

When we were leaving a woman opened the front of her dress and took out a baking of cold biscuits from right against her bare skin and gave them to me. The man told me to put them in my *shirt*, but I carried them in Manly's clean handkerchief instead. The man said it was hard for people to cook when traveling. They are very kind people. A pity to waste the biscuits but we could not eat them.

The Russians have a great huge dog. He was higher than my belt as we stood together and his great head looked like a wolf's, only larger. His ears were trimmed to make them like a wolf's ears and he was a bright brown all over. He was very loving, he rubbed against Rose and me and we put our arms around his big neck. There was a little puppy just like him and Manly tried to buy it but they would not sell.

They have splendid barns and great corn cribs and a windmill. Their land runs along the river. Each man works his own land but all of them together own all the stock in common.

We have spent a most pleasant Sunday and we are rested. Paul climbed onto Little Pet's back and the colt did not care, he was gentle.

July 23

We started at 8. Hated to leave our camping place, it seems quite like home. We crossed the James River and in 20 minutes we reached the top of the bluffs on the other side. We all stopped and looked back at the scene and I wished for an artist's hand or a poet's brain or even to be able to tell in good plain prose how beautiful it was. If I had been the Indians I would have scalped more white folks before I ever would have left it.

We could see the river winding down the valley, the water gleaming through the trees that grow on the bank. Beyond it the bluffs rose high and bare, browned and burned, above the lovely green of trees and grass and the shining water. On this side the bluffs again were gigantic brown waves tumbled and tossed about.

On this side of the James we have passed fields of corn 8 feet high. There are cottonwood hedges along the road, the trees 10 inches through and 35 or 40 feet tall. But it all seems burned and bare after our camping grounds by the river.

10 o'clock. It is 101° in the shade in the wagon, and hardly a breath of air.

At 11 o'clock, 9 miles from Yankton, we stopped at a windmill to water the horses. The man who owned the house told us he paid $5,000. for three 80's, without a building.

Not far from Yankton we crossed a bone-dry creek bed with the most desolate barren bluffs on each side. Covered with stones and the grass dry and brown, they looked like great drifts of sand that somehow had stopped drifting.

We reached Yankton at 4 o'clock. Drove by the insane asylum. The buildings look nice and they stand in the middle of a large farm of acres and acres of corn and potatoes. Manly wanted to stop and go through the asylum but I could not bear to, so we did not. We passed by the Yankton College, the buildings are very nice.

I am greatly disappointed in Yankton, it is a stick in the mud. We drove all over the town to find a little feed for the teams, went to the mill and the elevator and the feed stores, and finally found a couple of sacks of ground feed but not a bit of flax* in the whole town. There were no green vegetables, nor any figs nor dates in the grocery stores. It would be a blessing to Yankton if Carpenter would move down here, or if folks in Yankton would send to De Smet for what they need. They have a number of elevators, 2 or 3 mills, and 6 feed stores, but we carried the most of the feed away in two sacks.

I got my revolver fixed, then we had to spend so much time hunting for feed all over town that Mr.

---

* Flaxseed was indispensable first aid to hurts and minor ills. A boiling-hot flaxseed poultice holds hotter heat longer than a bread-and-milk one, and usually it works better than layers of cold vinegar-and-brown-paper.   R.W.L.

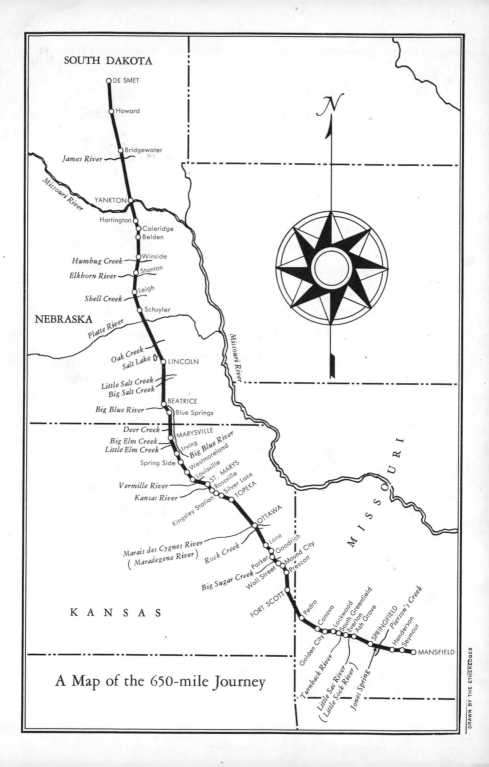

SOUTH DAKOTA

DE SMET

Howard

Bridgewater

James River

Missouri River

YANKTON

Hartington
Coleridge
Belden

Winside
Humbug Creek
Elkhorn River Stanton

Leigh
Shell Creek

NEBRASKA Schuyler

Platte River

Oak Creek
Salt Lake LINCOLN

Little Salt Creek
Big Salt Creek

Missouri River

BEATRICE
Big Blue River Blue Springs

Deer Creek MARYSVILLE
Big Elm Creek Irving
Little Elm Creek *Big Blue River*
Westmoreland
Spring Side Louisville
ST. MARYS
Rossville
Vermille River Silver Lake
Kansas River TOPEKA
Kingsley Station

OTTAWA

Lane
Rock Creek Goodrich

Marais des Cygnes River
(*Maradegene River*) Parker Mound City
Wall Street Prescott
Big Sugar Creek

MISSOURI

K A N S A S FORT SCOTT

Pedro
Canova
Golden City Lockwood
Everton South Greenfield
Ash Grove SPRINGFIELD
Pierson's Creek
Henderson
Seymour
MANSFIELD

Turnback River
Little Sac River
(*Little Sock River*)
Jones Spring

A Map of the 650-mile Journey

DRAWN BY THE ETHEREDGES

Cooley got to the ferry first. Mrs. Cooley and Paul crossed the river, then the ferry came back and took Mr. Cooley over. It was leaving just as we drove down to the landing at 6 o'clock and while we were waiting for it to come back a bad-looking storm came up. It was not rain, only wind and dust.

We had to face the river to keep the wagon's back to the wind so that it would not be blown over. The wind lifted the hind wheels twice before Manly could get them roped down. The ferryman did not like to try to cross the river in the storm. He waited on the other side until the blow was over, and we were afraid he would not cross again that night. But he did.*

Where we crossed the Missouri it is one mile wide, very nasty and muddy. I do not wonder that it is called

---

* When the rear wheels lifted as if the wagon were going end over end into the river, my father jumped out, leaving the reins in my mother's hands. While she held and gentled the nervous horses, I craned around the edge of the side-curtain to see what my father was doing. He was driving a picket-pin into the ground, and tying a wheel to it with the picket rope. Behind us was a covered wagon, behind it another, and another. As far as I could see, covered wagons stood one beyond another in a long, long line. Behind them and over them, high over half the sky, a yellow wave of dust was curling and coming. My mother said to me, "That's your last sight of Dakota."   R.W.L.

The Big Muddy, and since I have seen the dust blowing into it I do not think it strange that it is muddy. The Missouri is nothing like as beautiful as the Jim.

Pet made no fuss at all at the ferry, but drove onto it nicely, stood as quiet as could be, and calmly drove off it. Her colt Little Pet ran onto it loose and stood beside her as still as a mouse.

About a mile from the river we camped in woods. Temperature 98°.

July 24

Mr. Cooley got up early and went fishing but did not get a bite. We were all tired from being up so late last night, and did not get started until 9 o'clock. We had taken the wrong road, so we had to go back to the river and start again on the right one. For a little way we followed the river and could see down it, four or five miles across the water. It was a grand sight, though the scenery on the banks is nothing.

What is it about water that always affects a person? I never see a great river or lake but I think how I would like to see a world made and watch it through all its changes.

The banks of the Missouri are crumbling all the time

and falling into the water. In one place the road had fallen in. There on the river flats before we reached the bluffs we saw 24 hay stacks at one time, and mowing had only begun. Four mowing machines were working. Hay is $9. a ton in Yankton.

Well, we have come to the bluffs. On the side next the river they look as if they had been cut straight down with a knife. Grass has not grown on the face. All along the foot of it trees are growing, sheltered from the south wind. Plums, grapes, black currants and sweet clover grow wild on the bottom land. Sweet clover 8 feet high. And the first oak trees we have seen.

We have been going over the bluffs, the most desolate bare hills I ever saw, without houses or fields or trees and hardly any grass. Manly said he would just as soon own the whole of Nebraska as not, if it were fenced. Judging from all he has ever seen of the state it might do for pasture if he did not keep much stock. So far Nebraska reminds me of Lydia Locket's pocket, nothing in it, nothing on it, only the binding round it.

We meet covered wagons going north. Manly talked to a couple of men traveling from Kansas to South Dakota. They said there is nothing in Kansas.

The hens are laying yet. Temperature 110°.

We spent the night among the Nebraska hills, down in a hollow where they shut us in, and not a house in sight. This morning I like to look at the hills, there is something fascinating in their loneliness.

We started at 7:35. It is a nice cool morn. Went through Hartington at 8:30. It is a nice town, I like it much better than Yankton though it is smaller. Passed through Coleridge at 12:30, not much of a place. The wind is blowing and the dust flying till we can hardly see. Talk about hard roads in Dakota, I never saw hard roads till now. The more I see of Nebraska the less I like it. We have been climbing over bluffs all day.

Just south of Coleridge there are 22 families that are going to start for Missouri in about 6 weeks, though this country is *very* thinly settled. One man said he has lived here for 6 years and has not seen a good crop yet.

We camped east of the town of Beldon one mile, but within sight of it, by a creek. Not so much as a bush to be seen. Manly did the chores so Mr. Cooley could go fishing. He caught 11 fish. Temperature 109°.

The man living near where we camped is working for a man in Sioux City who owns 3,000 acres of land here, in a body. 500 acres of it are in pasture and 250 in meadow.

Mr. Cooley went fishing again this morning and caught 2. We were on the road at 8:40. There has been plenty of rain right here and crops are *good*, corn, wheat and oats. But three miles west they have nothing. Land is $25. an acre here.

Met a load of emigrants at noon. They are going north. Thermometer 110° in shade.

This afternoon we met a family of emigrants, man, woman and two children. They had been to Missouri and are coming back. They started from Moody County, Dakota, the 8th of May and went to Taney County, Missouri. They stayed only 10 days and started back, have been on the road ever since. They would not live in Missouri if you gave them the whole of it. "Why, hardly any of the houses have windows in them, just holes, and lots of the women have never seen a railroad train nor an organ," and the land is awful stony. They think of stopping in Cedar County Nebraska.

Crops are poor since noon, country about as dry as Dakota. Went through Winside about 4 o'clock. Roads are awfully hilly and Mr. Cooley wishes we had kept farther west and gone to Columbus instead of Schuyler.

Crossed Humbug Creek and camped by the first

house south. The people are Germans and very nice, they gave us milk. Humbug Creek and Winside are well named only they should have spelled it Windside. We have faced a hot *hard* wind all day.

July 27

Started at 8:15. We have gone through Cedar County and nearly through Wayne County, Nebraska. We cannot tell when we come to a county line as we could in Dakota, the roads pay no attention to section lines but wander up and down and around the hills.

The soil in Wayne County is very fine and close, not exactly clay but clayey. The people here claim it is the best soil on earth to stand drought.

Crossed the line into Stanton County at 9. There are large pastures and the grain fields are all fenced. A good many sleek cattle are in sight. Cornfields are 3 miles long and as far back as you can see. There are a few groves. Wind blows hard but cool this morning.

At 10:20 we saw *an orchard with apples.*

The hills are covered with corn as far as eye can see, acres and acres of corn. Lots of groves. Nearly all the people are Germans. One gave Manly two large apples off his trees. He has a large orchard and the trees hang full.

Just passed a house where the man owns 540 acres of land and has 300 hogs.

A little farther on, a farm of 500 acres. The owner had 450 hogs and only 50 bushels of old corn. He says if it does not rain within 24 hours the tassels on the new crop will dry and he will not harvest a kernel of corn. The corn looks nice to us but I suppose the farmers here know. Their wheat only sold for 32 cents last year and it is 32 cents now.

We came into the Elkhorn valley at 1:45 and it is pretty, very level, with many groves and nice houses and natural timber along the river.

An emigrant team is behind us and every minute I expect to hear the usual, Where did you come from? Where are you going? How are the crops up your way? This never—hardly ever—fails.

Found an ear of corn 10 inches long, 7½ inches around.

Arrived at Stanton at 3 P.M. It is a good looking town, large pretty buildings, clean big houses with trees. People mostly Germans. German signs on the stores and German texts on the churches. Wheat is going 16 to 20 bushels to the acre. Corn is killed by the hot wind. Yesterday it was 126° in the shade here in Stanton.

Crossed the Elkhorn river on a bridge. A few miles farther on we camped by the side of the road in the shade of some trees. There was a gang of horse traders on the river and we did not want to camp near them.

July 28

We washed this morning, or rather Mrs. Cooley did out a washing and I washed 4 garments. I wash out the most of the clothes in a pail as they get dirty so I do not have washings. The neighbors sent us a pailful of delicious cold milk, out of the water where they keep it for the creamery.

The washing had to dry, so we did not start to travel until after dinner. The roads are awful killers for the horses. We had gone about 3 miles when we missed Cooleys' dog. Mr. Cooley wanted to go on but Mrs. Cooley would not. Finally it was decided that he would go back to look for her and the rest of us would go on.

We took the ridge road, not to go up and down the hills, so we followed along the top of the ridge through acres and acres of corn fields. We could see nothing of

Mr. Cooley when it was time to camp, but we camped by the side of the road on the prairie. There was good grass for the horses and a pump in a pasture, just through the fence.

We got the horses watered and picketed out, when here came Mr. Cooley over a hill from the south. An old Bohemian had come out and would not let him cross a field where we had gone, so he had to go all around to come back to us. He had found the dog where we camped last night.

The oats and wheat are good here and the corn does not look bad but of course it needs rain so people are blue and cross and stingy.

There are wild strawberry plants here, and rattle-snakes.

Sunday, July 29
Cooked breakfast and bathed and lay around in the shade of the wagons. Temperature 96°. Rested all day and went to bed early.

July 30
Started at 8 and crossed the line into Colfax County twenty minutes later. Went through Leigh at 10

o'clock, a lively little town that has not outgrown country.

Crops are still the same but roads are not so hilly.

We camped on the bank of Shell Creek in the woods. A lovely place, even better than our camp on the Jim river. The children and Mrs. Cooley and I went wading. The bank was so steep that we had to steady each other down, and pull and push each other up. We paddled and played in the rippling cool water. Rose sat down in it, splash! We found two large live clams.

July 31

The wind blew terribly in the night. We were thankful for the shelter of the trees. It must have rained hard somewhere, for the creek raised 8 inches.

Started at 9. We are following down the valley of the creek on a nice level road.

Reached Schuyler at noon, all the way on the level road. Here we had to get the tires set, so we did not leave town till 3. I met an interesting woman. She drove up to the wagon in a buggy and began by asking if it isn't hot to be traveling. I liked her and we talked a long time. Her husband owns a large farm north of Schuyler but they are going back to the West Indies in a few weeks. They are Canadians but her husband was

36

in the West Indies when a boy and they have spent half their lives there. They thought they would like to live here but do not like it as well as they expected, so they will rent the farm again and she thinks they will stay in the West Indies when they get there. She said it is a monotonous life but very pleasant, the servants do all the work. She wanted to know all about Dakota and everything she said was sensible. She is an elderly lady, and I think Scotch.

South of Schuyler the land is sandy, two miles to La Platte river. We crossed the Platte on a bridge half a mile long, humped in the middle so we went up and down hill on it. The river is full of sand bars that keep shifting.

Half a mile beyond it we camped in a grove of willows. The Cooleys lingered in town and had not arrived when we camped. Manly and I hurried our supper and left Rose to watch the camp while we "hit the dust" back to the river so I could go wading in daylight.

The water was clear, warm and soft. The sand was soft and warm but shifting. It ran away right under my feet while I waded, or if I stood still it drifted over them. For fun I stood still until my feet were covered. As Manly said, we "hit the dust" going, but we "packed sand" coming back.

The wooden bridge across the Platte River,

Schuyler, Nebraska, as it looked when we crossed it.

On the way back we saw a snake and two large toads. We went into a pasture to look at some trees. The sand had drifted away from them until the tree trunks stood up higher than my head, tiptoe on their bare, gnarled roots. I could walk under those trees, between their roots, by stooping just a little.

August 1

It rained a little in the night. We started at 8:40 and the road was level till noon but terribly hilly all the afternoon. We camped by Oak Creek in a little natural glade among the oaks, the best camp yet.

August 2

Started late because of a lame horse, one of Mr. Cooley's. They had to take care of her foot. We met a team of movers going to work out the railroad tax.* Camped early, only a little way from Oak Creek.

---

* I suppose this was a local or State tax to pay a subsidy to a railroad builder. Railroads were the fastest, most modern transportation. The Lincoln administration began to subsidize them from taxes in the 1860's. States and localities, even small towns, followed the example eagerly in the 1880's–90's. "Working out taxes" at $1 a day was usual. R.W.L.

Started at 9. Good level road into Lincoln, the capital of Nebraska and a beautiful large city. It is two miles from the first hotel to the post office. The County Court House and the Capitol are grand buildings, and so is the penitentiary. We saw two prisoners in their striped clothes standing outside the gate in the wall. A carload of new barrels was on a sidetrack beside them, I suppose made by the prisoners. A high stone wall surrounds several buildings and joins the back of the main building. Smaller buildings inside the wall look like workshops, one like a foundry.

Eight emigrant wagons trailed our three through several streets of the city. There are motor street-cars in Lincoln. Pet and Little Pet were not afraid of them but they scared Mrs. Cooley's team so that they plunged up a bank and nearly upset her wagon.* But it came out all right.

We crossed 11 creeks today, or one creek 11 times, I

* Paul was not allowed to drive through cities and other dangerous places. His mother came back to their second wagon then and took the lines and the responsibility away from him. He was humiliated and I felt hotly (in silence) this injustice to him. He drove the big team perfectly all the rest of the way. George rode with him, but Paul was responsible for the second team and wagon. R.W.L.

don't know which, and we passed Salt Lake north west of Lincoln. We are camped about a mile from the penitentiary. Temperature 74°.

August 4

On the road at 7:45, a nice level road and good farms fenced with board fences. We are following the tele-graph wires to Beatrice, then do not follow the railroad but go across country.

We have crossed Little Salt Creek and Big Salt Creek. Orchards are as common here as houses. Manly traded one fire mat for a whole bushel of large ripe apples. Plums are nearly ripe. Crops look splendid to us but everyone tells Manly that they are very poor and will make no grain to mention. We passed the best field of oats that Manly ever saw.

Made a hard long drive to get to a good camp, and when we got there we found the creek dry and no grass but plenty of sand burs. Camped in the edge of a town.

Sunday, August 5

Same as last Sunday. Saw five emigrant wagons. Lost the thermometer.

Started at 8:30 and reached Beatrice at noon. Corn all dried up and no ears on it. Oats and wheat threshed and a great deal of plowing done.

Beatrice is not as large as Lincoln but a nice town, I think. We saw the courthouse, it is handsome.

Splendid roads all day. We crossed Blue River just south of Beatrice, drove through Blue Springs at 5 in the afternoon and crossed Blue River again. Did not see much of the city because we drove along the north edge and down the east side past a big mill run by water-power. The river runs east of the town, a very pretty river. I do not mention orchards any more because they are common here, there are so many of them.

We saw 8 acres of seedling apple trees about 12 inches high near Blue Springs. Today has been quite cool, but with a little too much wind.

August 7

On the road at 7:30, we crossed the line into Kansas at 10:28¼ exactly. Judging from what we have seen and heard of Nebraska, the south east corner is quite a good country, but taken as a whole it is "nix good." I don't like Nebraska.

Crossed Deer Creek at 11 o'clock. At 4 in the afternoon we came to Marysville, the county seat of Marshall County, on the Blue river. Here there is a watermill, capacity 300 barrels a day. We saw many nice houses and two palatial residences in the town. Around one is a massive brick fence about 5 feet high, thick and strong looking. On each side of the front gate a large granite lion is crouching, and on each side of the side gate a large granite dog is lying down.

Beyond Marysville we saw an acre of sweet potatoes, large dark green leaves on vines covering the ground.

We drove 27 miles today and camped near a house where there were two men drunk. They had lost the bars off their wagon, wanted to trade horses, etc. Manly had a time getting rid of them without offense.

August 8

Started at 8:30. Soon crossed Little Elm Creek and Big Elm Creek and drove through beautiful woods of elm, oak, ash, hickory, butternut and walnut. Wild plums, grapes and currants are abundant, and briars and wild flowers of all kinds. A rich sight.

Crossed Blue river again, a lovely river, so clean

always, and fresh and cool. We crossed it on a bridge. This bridge is about 300 feet long. Irving is a tiny small town but it has an Opera House with a round roof, it looks like an engine boiler.

Then we crossed the Blue again. Every time we cross it, it is lovelier than before. Improved land here is from $15. to $25. an acre. Could buy an 80 on the Blue bottoms, well improved, for $3,000. The bottom land is all good farms. The bluffs are stony.

We camped near Spring Side, well named. There are springs on every side. I got water from a spring that boils up out of solid rock, cool and clear.

August 9

Started at 8:30. Awfully hilly roads, and stony. We saw a milk-house built of stone with a spring running through it, a splendid thing. Land in Pottawatomie County is $4. an acre up.

Camped in the edge of Westmoorland, the county seat. At supper time we had company, some men, two women, and children. They are regular southerners, camped near by, traveling north. To Nebraska or maybe Dakota, looking for work.

Marysville, Kansas. This is a "German Day" parade,

GORDON HOHN, MARYSVILLE, KANSAS

which may have taken place in the year we were there.

Started at 8:30 and drove through the driest country we have seen since leaving Dakota. Went through Louisville, drove 3 miles farther and camped on the bank of Vermille River, some call it Stony Creek.

Today was not as monotonous as common. 3 emigrant wagons passed us going south, and one going north. Manly and Mr. Cooley took turns talking to the people. Five wagons were going to Missouri or Arkansas, one to Arkansas, one to Indian Territory.

We had a good camping place on a little headland by the river. I rode Little Pet awhile, bareback, not going anywhere—she was turned loose to feed. Two emigrants talked to me, a young man and his mother in their wagon. They used to live in Missouri, went to Colorado, are now going back to Missouri to stay.

Drove through St. Mary's. A pleasant town but strange, it is altogether southern, and Catholic. There is a beautiful large church with a pure white marble

Saint Mary above the wide doors and two white marble statues of Mother and Child in the yard. The houses are neat and pretty. It is a clean town.

We drove to the top of a little bluff to look over the Kansas River, and there on the bottom lands we saw cornfields stretching as far as the eye could reach. Manly said he should think there were a thousand acres in sight.

On our way Manly went to a farmhouse to trade a fire mat for some green corn for our supper, and we had an invitation to stay to dinner and put our horses in the barn and feed them. The woman came out to make me welcome. Such nice people, and a nice place, everything well kept up. Of course we could not stay. We could not be neighborly to them in return and we must get to Missouri and settled before winter.

At noon we went through Rossville, a small place, but just as we were going by the depot the train came in. The engine frightened Prince and he went through a barb-wire fence. He struck it straight and went right through it, end over end, jumped up, ran against a clothesline and broke that and ran back to the fence. He stopped when Manly said, "Whoa, Prince," and Manly helped him through the wire. He had only one mark, a cut about an inch long where a barb had struck him. How he ever got through so well is a wonder.

Watermelons are ripe and plentiful. Manly and Mr. Cooley bought big ones for 5 cents. We stopped by the road in the shade of trees and all of us had all the watermelon we could eat.

We passed Kingsley Station, 80 miles west of Kansas City, Missouri, and 558 miles east of Denver, Colorado. Went through Silver Lake. The lake itself is south of the town; it is 4 miles long and a half a mile wide, and trees are all around it. There is a place where a man rents boats.

We camped in a schoolhouse yard. There was a hedge all around it and a pump by the house, besides a sycamore tree. Two families going by in covered wagons stopped for water. They had been to Missouri and were going back home to dispose of their property in Nebraska, then they are moving to Missouri.

It is *terribly* dusty. We breathe dust all day and everything is covered thick with it.

August 14

Started at 8:30. Dust is 3 to 5 inches deep on the road and the breeze is on our backs so all the time we are in a smother of dust. Along the roads are hedges of Osage Orange trees, 20 or 30 feet high, set close together. They are thorny. Their fruit is like green oranges, but no good to eat nor for anything else.

We stopped to eat dinner about a mile from Topeka, then drove on through the city. There are a great many colored people in and around it. In North Topeka the street cars are electric, in South Topeka they are motor cars.

The streets are asphaltum pavement and it is lovely to drive on, so soft and quiet that it doesn't seem real. It gives like rubber to the horses' feet. The caulks on their shoes make dents in it and slowly the dents fill up till the place is smooth again.

We drove a block out of our way to see the Capitol, where they had that war in the legislature. The building is handsome but the grounds are all unkempt, not finished at all.

We crossed the Kansas River on an iron bridge that must be 400 or 500 feet long. The river is like the Platte, not quite as wide but full of sand bars.

South of Topeka a man gave us some late daily papers. He has 240 acres here but his home is in Colorado. He has mining interests there. He told Manly that

Kansas Avenue in Topeka, Kansas,

the fuss over silver in Washington has made him lose $1,000,000.

We camped by the side of a church, in dust.

Started at 7:20. Found a little black-and-tan dog in the road, lost. He is skin and bones, must have been starving, and is afraid of us. We stopped at several houses to ask, but nobody knew where he belonged so we are taking him along. The children delight to feed him milk. We have named him Fido.

Today I saved a horse chestnut, and we came to hazel nuts for the first time.

Went through Richland at noon. We drove past the church. There was a Sunday School picnic on the church grounds.

We camped by a schoolhouse in the southwest corner of Douglas County. There was good grass for the teams and a pump gushed out delicious cold, clear water. This is the best farming country we have seen yet, prairie with natural groves here and there and timber along the creeks.

As we came along the road Manly sold and traded a good many fire mats, and one farmer wanted to rent him a farm for a third of the crops. Another came to us

it looked when we passed through.

at the schoolhouse where we camped, and wanted us to stay here and rent. We are going on to Missouri but may come back here if we do not like it there. Land here is worth $20. to $40. an acre.

August 16

On our way at 7:25. Fido is quite friendly this morning, he still seems sad but he has stopped trembling and seems content to sit in my lap and look at the country we are passing. The wheat crop is bountiful here and the corn crop is pretty good. There is a coal bank where men mine the coal and sell all they dig for $1.25 a ton.

At 5 in the afternoon we came through Ottawa. There is a North and a South Ottawa, separated by the Maradegene River. They are the county seat of Franklin County. The men of Ottawa stole the county seat in the night, from another town, and for some time they had to guard it with the militia, to keep it. The court house is quite an imposing building.

The Sante Fe Railroad hospital is in the north edge of North Ottawa, a large brick building. It looks very clean. In South Ottawa there is a handsome college building made of the native stone. In all the towns now there are many colored people.

We camped on the bank of Rock Creek in the suburbs of South Ottawa. Two men coming by stopped and looked at Prince for some time and as they went on the elderly one said to the other, "That is the nicest colt I have seen for years." The hens are laying yet.

August 17

Fido is a good watch dog. He growls at every stranger who comes to the wagon, and at night at everyone that passes.

We started at 7:30. The wild morning-glories are rioting everywhere, all colors like the tame ones. We passed a large field of castor beans. They are raised here as a crop, they run 10 to 15 bushels to the acre and sell for $1.25 to $1.50 a bushel. They are picked every two weeks, piled up in the sun till they pop open, then run through a fanning mill and sacked.

We reached Lane at 4 o'clock and had old Pet shod. The blacksmith came from Kentucky two years ago and looks just like the pictures of a Kentucky man. He has 130 acres of bottom land running down to Pottawatomie River, and a stone house as large as any house in De Smet. It is very handsome and perfectly finished. The house stands on Main Street in Lane and the land lies northwest from it. He is going back to Kentucky and wants to sell. Asks $4,300. for shop, house and land.

South of Lane we stopped at a farmhouse to ask for water and the woman said she did not have enough to spare but we could get a plenty "over yon way."

Camped again by a schoolhouse and pump. Washed out some things after supper. They dry overnight.

August 18

Started at 7 this morning, went through Goodrich and came to Parker at noon. They are both small places and the country around them is not as good as we have been seeing. The people say they never have the rain here that others get farther north.

Camped by Big Sugar Creek, up on its high bank in the woods beside the road.

Sunday, August 19

Mr. Cooley's stove had worked loose. He and Manly had to fix it so it will ride. Mrs. Cooley and I and the children went down to the creek and found some mussels and some clam shells. A woman and 2 children came to see us. They come from Missouri and they are camping near by on their way to Nebraska.

August 20

Got a good start at 7:30 but the roads are awfully stony. Crops are poor. Everyone tells us they never get rain here when they need it. We went through Wall Street, it is nothing but a little country store. At noon we came to Mound City which is quite a city. We bought bread and an 8-cent pie and 2 cents worth of tomatoes. Tomatoes are 30 cents a bushel.

We stopped to eat dinner in the shade of a tree beside the road. Three emigrant wagons passed while we were eating. Two were going to Missouri and one coming back. This afternoon we saw three more, one going to Missouri, one coming back. Manly did not ask the other.

Water has been scarce all day and what little we found tasted so bad we could not get a good drink. It is clear and clean but it feels slick and tastes bitter, it spoils the taste of tea. The horses have to be very thirsty to take it.

Camped beside the road on the prairie. Bought a little hay and could get only a little water. Looks like rain.

August 21

It rained hard most of the night and was still pouring down when time came to get up. Manly put on his rubber coat, started the fire and put water on to heat, then fed our horses. By that time the rain was no more than a drizzle so I got out and made breakfast. We ate in the wagon, out of the wet.

Roads are muddy but sky is clear overhead. We went through Prescott, only a little station. Met a family of emigrants who have spent the last two months traveling in southwest Missouri. They do not like it at all down there. The man said, "Right there is the place to go if man wants to bury himself from the world and live on hoecake and clabber," and the woman agreed with him.

We passed another covered wagon stopped by the road, and those folks are on their way to Missouri. The whole country is just full of emigrants, going and coming. Fort Scott seemed to be crowded with them. We reached Fort Scott at 6 o'clock, and a man there said that 15 emigrant wagons went along that street yesterday.

Fort Scott is a bower of trees. The houses look clean and contented; the business buildings are handsome. The country around Fort Scott looks like it might be a very good country. Crops are good where there are any, but there is lots of idle land and many places are gone back. It seems that the people are shiftless; but you never can

The main street of Fort Scott, Kansas,

as it looked in the late 1880's.

tell. A man said this country is worthless, and when Manly said that it looked to him like good land, he said, Oh yes, the land will raise anything that's planted but if you can't sell what you raise for enough to pay back the cost of raising it, what's the land worth?

Coal is lying around on top of the ground and cropping out of every bank. At the coal mines, or coal banks as they call them, the coal is worth $5. a bushel.

We received 3 letters at Fort Scott, 2 from home. A little way south of the city we camped beside the road.

August 22

A good start at 7:15 and this morning we are driving through pretty country. Crops look good. Oats are running 30 to 60 bushels to the acre, wheat from 10 to 30. All the wood you want can be had for the hauling and coal is delivered at the house for $1.25 a ton. Land is worth from $10. an acre up, unimproved, and $15. to $25. when well improved, 12 miles from Fort Scott.

Exactly at 2:24¾ P.M. we crossed the line into Missouri. And the very first cornfield we saw beat even those Kansas cornfields.

We met 7 emigrant wagons leaving Missouri. One family had a red bird, a mocking bird, and a lot of canaries in cages hung under the canvas in the wagon with them. We had quite a chat and heard the mocking-bird sing. We camped by a house in the woods.

Started out at 7:30. The country looks nice this morning. At 9:35 we came to Pedro, a little town on one side of the railroad tracks, and just across the tracks on the other side is the town of Liberal. A man in Pedro told us that one of the finest countries in the world will be around Mansfield.

In the late afternoon we went through Lamar, the nicest small city we have seen, 2,860 inhabitants. It is all so clean and fresh, all the streets set out to shade trees.

We camped among oak trees, not far from a camp of emigrants from Kentucky. Beautiful sturdy oak trees on both sides of the road.

August 24

On the road bright and early, 7:20. Weather cool and cloudy, looks like rain. Went through Canova in the morning. It is a little place. At noon we were going through Golden City, a nicer little place. The country looks good, but judging from weeds in the gardens and fields, the people are shiftless. This is a land of many springs and clear brooks. Some of the earth is yellow and some is red. The road is stony often.

Went through another little town, Lockwood, at 4 o'clock, and camped by a swift-running little creek of the clearest water. It is most delicious water to drink, cold, with a cool, snappy flavor.

Except in the towns, we have seen only one schoolhouse so far in Missouri.

We drove in the rain this afternoon, for the first time since we left Dakota. It was a good steady pouring rain, but we kept dry in the wagon and the rain stopped before camping time.

August 25

Left camp at 7:35. It rained again in the night and the road was muddy but after a few miles we came to country where it did not rain so the road was dry. The uplands are stony but there are good bottomland farms. Much timber is in sight, oaks, hickories, walnuts, and there are lots of wild crabapples, plums and thorn apples.

In South Greenfield two land agents came out and wanted us to stop here. One was C. C. Akin, the man who located Mr. Sherwin. He said Mr. Sherwin was here only a week ago, has just gone. Mr. Sherwin looked Wright County over thoroughly and came back to Cedar County and located here. But finally Mr. Akin said there is just as good land in Wright County as Mr. Sherwin bought.

Well, we are in the Ozarks at last, just in the beginning of them, and they are beautiful. We passed along the foot of some hills and could look up their sides. The trees and rocks are lovely. Manly says we could almost live on the looks of them.

We stopped for dinner just before we came to the prettiest part, by the side of a swiftly running stream, Turnback River. We forded it, through the shallow water all rippling and sparkling.

There was another clear stream to cross before we came to Everton at 5 o'clock. Here we stopped to get the horses shod but there was not time to shoe them all today, so we camped by a creek in the edge of town for over Sunday.

Sunday, August 26

A day for writing, reading, sleeping. We let the children wade in the shallow creek, within our sight. I spent almost the whole time writing to the home folks about the country since Fort Scott and these hills and woods.

August 27

Out of camp at 7:10. We like this country. A man tried to get us to settle just across the road from him, said we could buy that 40 for $700. It was good land.

We forded Little Sock River and came through Ash Grove, a lively little town noted for its lime kiln. Two new brick blocks are going up on Main Street.

Camped 12 miles from Springfield. Manly was un-hitching the team when a man with his wife and daughter in a covered wagon drove up and wanted to know where he could water his mules. They live 14 miles east of Springfield in Henderson County and were going to visit the woman's brother in Ash Grove.

After we had talked awhile they said they would like to camp by us if we could sell them a little meat to cook. They had not intended to camp and had brought nothing to eat. We let them have some meat and they used our camp stove, so we got quite well acquainted. They are good, friendly folks. Their name is Davis. After the chores were done they brought over a large watermelon and we called the Cooleys to come, and all of us ate the whole big melon. You can buy a 20-lb. watermelon here for 5 cents.

Left camp at 6:28. Good road from Ash Grove all the way to Springfield, not hilly nor very stony. This is the Ozark plateau and the country looks much like prairie country though there are groves and timber always along the streams.

Arrived in Springfield at 9:25. It is a thriving city with fine houses and four business blocks stand around a town square. The stores are well stocked and busy. Manly hitched the horses and we bought shoes for Rose and myself, a calico dress for me, and a new hat for Manly. It did not take much time and we drove right along through the city. We were out of it before noon. It has 21,850 inhabitants, and is the nicest city we have seen yet. It is simply grand.

We could see two straight miles down Walnut street, a very little down grade, with large shade trees on each side, large handsome residences, and the pavement as smooth and clean as can be.

Five miles east of Springfield is Jones spring. The water is clear as glass, and it comes pouring out of a cave in a ledge of rock. At its mouth the cave is 4 feet high and 10 feet wide, and nobody knows how far back it goes. Manly and Mr. Cooley went quite a distance back into it and threw stones as far as they could throw them, and the stones fell plunk into water far back in the dark.

The water pours out of the cave 14 inches deep and runs away over the stones among the trees, a lively little creek.

We were told that 7 miles southeast of Jones spring a stream comes out of a cave so large that you can keep rowing a boat back into it for half a day.

After crossing Pierson's Creek we met, one day after another, 10 emigrant wagons leaving Missouri. We camped in the edge of Henderson, a little inland town, on the bank of a spring brook.

August 29

Left camp at 7:10. We are driving along a lively road through the woods, we are shaded by oak trees. The farther we go, the more we like this country. Parts of Nebraska and Kansas are well enough but Missouri is simply glorious. There Manly interrupted me to say, "This is beautiful country."

The road goes up hill and down, and it is rutted and dusty and stony but every turn of the wheels changes our view of the woods and the hills. The sky seems lower here, and it is the softest blue. The distances and the valleys are blue whenever you can see them. It is a drowsy country that makes you feel wide awake and alive but somehow contented.

We went through a little station on the railroad and a few miles farther on we came to a fruit farm of 400 acres. A company owns it. There are 26,000 little young trees already set out in rows striping the curves of the land, and the whole 400 acres will be planted as soon as possible. Acres of strawberries and other small fruit are in bearing. We stopped to look our fill of the sight and Manly fell into conversation with some of the company's men. They told him of a 40 he can buy for $400., all cleared and into grass except five acres of woods, and with a good ever-flowing spring, a comfortable log house and a barn.

We drove through Seymour in the late afternoon. The Main Streets of towns here are built around open squares, with the hitching posts surrounding the square. In the office of the Seymour paper, the Enterprise, a girl was setting type. A man spoke to us, who had lived 14 years in Dakota, near Sioux Falls, he has a brother living there now. He is farming near Seymour. He said the climate here can't be beat, we never will want to leave these hills, but it will take us some time to get used to the stones.

Oh no, we are not out of the world nor behind the times here in the Ozarks. Why, even the cows know "the latest." Two of them feeding along the road were playing Ta-ra-ra *Boom!* de-ay! The little cow's bell rang Ta-ra-ra, then the bigger cow's bell clanged, *Boom!* de-ay. I said, "What is that tune they are playing?" and we listened. It was as plain as could be, tones and time and all, and so comical. We drove on singing Ta-ra-ra *Boom!* de-ay! along the road.

We passed several springs and crossed some little brooks. The fences are snake fences of split logs and all along them, in the corners, fruit grows wild. There are masses of blackberries, and seedling peaches and plums and cherries, and luscious-looking fruits ripening in little trees that I don't know,* a lavishness of fruit growing wild. It seems to be free for the taking.

We could not reach Mansfield today. Camped by a

* These were wild persimmons and pawpaws.   R.W.L.

Mansfield, Missouri, as it looked about 1894. This picture wa

spring 10½ miles short of it. In no time at all Rose and I filled a quart pail with big juicy blackberries. They are growing wild in big patches in the woods, ripening and falling off and wasting.

Six more emigrant wagons camped around the spring before dark. Seasoned oak wood, sawed, split and delivered and corded, brings $1. a cord here.

August 30, 1894

Hitched up and going at 7:10. The road is rough and rocky through the ravines but not so bad between them and there are trees all the way.

We are passing through the Memphis fruit farms, 1,500 acres, part of the way on both sides of the road. It is a young orchard, rows upon rows of little trees, apple and peach, curving over the plowed hills.

Some covered wagons came up behind us and we came up behind some ahead, all the teams going slowly, holding back down hill and pulling up hill. At 11:30 we came into Mansfield in a long line of 10 emigrant wagons.

Mansfield is a good town of 300 or 400 inhabitants in a good central location where it should grow fast. The railroad runs on one side of the square and two stage-

probably taken on Memorial Day or on the Fourth of July.

coach lines go from the depot, one south to the County seat of Douglas County, the other north to the County seat of Wright County. There is everything here already that one could want though we must do our worshipping without a Congregational church. There is a Methodist church and a Presbyterian. There is a good school. Around the Square, two general stores, two drug stores, the bank, a Boston Racket store, livery stable, blacksmith shop near. There are several nice large houses in big yards with trees. South of the tracks is as good as north of them; two or three big houses, and a flour mill is there by a mill pond.

Camped in the woods in the western edge of town and this afternoon Manly looked over one place for sale but was not exactly suited.

*　　*　　*　　*

III

Here my mother's record ends. Fifty years later I began casually to speak of our camp in those vanished woods and she stopped the words in my mouth with a fierce, "I don't want to *think* of it!"

I do not remember how many days my father spent hunting for land that the secret hundred dollar bill would buy. Every morning he rode away with some land agent to limp up and down the hills and to come back at evening, nothing found yet.

Paul and George and I were joyous. After the long boredom of so many dull days that we hardly remembered De Smet, now every day was Sunday without Sunday's clean clothes and staid behavior. The camp was a Sunday camp; the Cooleys' wagons on one side, ours on the other; in the grove between them the table and chairs were set and the hammock hung in the shade. The camp stove stood a little way apart over cooling ashes. Farther away the horses were tied under the trees, and behind the wagons were screened places for our Saturday baths.

We must stay within sight or at least within hearing if our mothers called us, but as soon as morning tasks were done we were free to play in the woods. All day we climbed trees, picked berries, ate unripe walnuts and hazel nuts, cracked between two stones. We startled rabbits that we must not chase far; we watched squirrels and birds, beetles and anthills. The hot air was full of good smells of rotting logs, dusty weeds, damp underneaths of mats of last year's oakleaves. Dandelion stems curled bitter on my tongue's tip and the green curls wilted over my ears.

Sharp flat stones were thick underfoot; we stubbed our toes on them and all our big toes were wrapped in rags. Stone-bruises on our summer-calloused heels didn't stop our running. We found toadstools and mosses like teeny-tiniest forests, flat greenish-gray lichen on rocks, little perfect skins of locusts, empty, thin and brittle, clinging with tiny claws to the bark of trees.

We picked up strange stones. When I showed my father a thin triangular one, wavy all over and sharp-pointed, he said it was an Indian arrowhead. We collected dozens of them and Paul found a stone ax-head.

One day I had to stay in camp with Mrs. Cooley, I must mind her and not go out of her sight. My father had found a place, my mother was going with him to see it, and they wanted no worry about me while they were gone. There never had been such a long morning. I was embarrassed and so was Mrs. Cooley. When at last I saw the team coming, my father and mother coming back, I felt like exploding; I could hardly be still and not speak until spoken to.

My father was glowing and my mother shining. She never had talked so fast. Just what they wanted, she told Mrs. Cooley, so much, much more than they'd hoped for. A year-round spring of the best water you ever drank, a snug log house, in woods, on a hill, only a mile and a half from town so Rose could walk to school, and to cap all, just think! four hundred young apple trees, heeled in, all ready to set out when the land was cleared. They'd bought it, as soon as dinner was over they were going to the bank to sign the papers. We were moving out that afternoon.

When he was excited my father always held himself quiet and steady, moving and speaking with deliberation. Sometimes my quick mother flew out at him, but this day she was soft and warm. She left him eating at the camp table, told me to clear it and wash the dishes when he was through, and went into the screened place to get ready to meet the banker.

I perched on a stump and watched her brush out her hair and braid it. She had beautiful hair, roan-brown, very fine and thick. Unbraided, it shimmered down to her heels; it was so long that when it was tightly braided she could sit on the braids. Usually it hung down her back in one wide braid but when she dressed up she must put up her hair and endure the headache.

Now she wound the braid around and around into a big mass on the back of her head, and fastened it with her tortoise-shell pins. She fluffed her bangs into a soft little mat in front, watching her comb in the small looking-glass fastened to a tree, and suddenly I realized that she was whistling; I remembered that I hadn't heard her whistling lately.

"Whistling girls and crowing hens always come to some bad ends," she'd say gaily. She was whistling always. She whistled like a bird whistling a tune, clear and soft, clear and sweet, trilling, chirping, or dropping notes one by one as a meadow lark drops them from the sky. I was pleased to hear her whistling again.

Whistling, she buttoned up her new shoes with the buttonhook. She took off her calico dress and folded it neatly. Standing in her bleached muslin petticoats and corset cover trimmed with crocheted lace, she took her best dress, her black cloth wedding dress, out of the box in which it had traveled from Dakota. Whistling, Oh Susanna, don't you cry for me, she put on the skirt and smoothed the placket. I was sorry that the skirt hid her new shoes. She coaxed her arms into the basque's tight sleeves and carefully buttoned all the glittery jet buttons up its front to her chin. With her gold pin she pinned the fold of ribbon, robin's-egg blue, to the front of the stand-up collar. Then, the very last thing, the climax: she pinned on her black sailor hat with the blue ribbon around the crown and the spray of wheat standing straight up at one side. The braids in back tilted the hat forward just a little; in front, the narrow brim rested on the mat of bangs.

She looked lovely; she was beautiful. You could see my father think so, when she came out and he looked at her.

She told him to hurry or they'd be late, but she spoke as if she were singing, not cross at all. He went into the screened place to change his shirt and comb his hair and mustache, and put on his new hat. To me my mother said that I could clear the table now, be sure to wash every dish while they were gone and, as usual, she told me to be careful not to break one. I never had broken a dish.

I remember all this so clearly because of what happened. I had taken away the dishes and wiped the table. My mother put down on it her clean handkerchief and her little red cloth pocketbook with the mother-of-pearl sides; she was wearing her kid gloves. Carefully she brought the writing desk and set it on the table. She laid back its slanted upper half and lifted out the narrow wooden tray that held the pen and the inkwell.

The hundred dollar bill was gone.

There was a shock, like stepping in the dark on a top step that isn't there. But it could not be true. It was true; the place in the desk was empty. Everything changed. In the tight strangeness my father and mother were not like them; I did not feel like me.

Two views of the lap desk which held the $100 bill.

They asked, Had I told someone? No. Had I never said anything to anyone, ever, about that money? No. Had I seen a stranger near the wagon when they were not there? No. Or in camp? No.

My mother said it wasn't possible; not the Cooleys. My father agreed, no, not them. It *must* be there. My mother had seen it last in Kansas.

They took every sheet of writing paper out of the desk and shook it; they took each letter out of its envelope, unfolded it, looked into the empty envelope. They turned the desk upside down and shook it, the felt-covered inside lids flapping. My mother said they were losing their senses. Suddenly she thought, hoped, asked, Had I taken it myself, to play with?

NO! I felt scalded. She asked, Was I sure? I hadn't just opened the desk sometime, for fun? My throat swelled shut; I shook my head, no. "Don't cry," she said automatically. I wouldn't cry, I never cried, I was angry, insulted, miserable, I was not a baby who'd play with money or open that desk for fun, I was going on eight years old. I was little, alone, and scared. My father and mother sat there, still. In the long stillness I sank slowly into nothing but terror, pure terror without cause or object, a nightmare terror.

Finally my mother said, "Well." She meant, No use crying over spilled milk. What can't be cured must be endured. My father told her not to blame herself, it wasn't her fault. Carefully she peeled off her thin kid gloves. She turned them right-side-out finger by finger, smoothed them. She said that he'd better go explain to the banker.

Somehow the worst was over when he tried to put it off, saying something might turn up, and she flared out that he knew as well as she did, "nothing turns up that we don't turn up ourselves." Then she told me to run away and play, and I remembered the unwashed dishes. She had forgotten them.

For days, I don't remember how many days, everything was the same as ever and not at all the same. I said nothing about the disaster; I didn't want to. My mother told Mrs. Cooley that they thought best to take time to make up their minds. My father looked for work in town. My mother knew nobody there. Mr. Cooley sold one of his teams and one wagon; and Paul and George were going to move into the hotel and help run it. I knew we could sell the horses, but what then? Covered wagons were going by every day, going both ways as usual, some camping overnight nearby. Often I tried to think what would happen when we had nothing to eat; I couldn't.

Blackberries were fewer now and smaller. I was deep in the briary patch, hunting them, when my mother called, and called again before I could get out without tearing my dress on the clutching thorns and run over the sharp stones to the camp. My father was hitching up, my mother was putting last things into the wagon. They had bought the farm. She had found the hundred dollar bill. In the writing desk. The jolting had slipped it into a crack in the desk and I was to stop asking questions and get into the wagon. Just as she was, my mother had found my father and gone to sign the papers, and just as I was, without even washing my feet, I was to obey her and get up onto that wagon seat, *now*, and no more words about it.

The town began with two small houses on a side road in the woods. Then there were two big houses in large yards with trees, and a cunning little low house right at the edge of the gravel sidewalk. On the other side of the road, opposite the little house, stairs went up the side of the hotel where Paul and George would live. In front of the hotel was the Square, with trees in it and lines of hitching posts around it, except on the far side where the railroad track was. We were driving along Main Street, and it was on one side of us and in front of us and behind us, too; it went around three sides of the Square. It was three solid rows of stores behind three high board sidewalks. This was The Gem City of the Ozarks.

We passed a big Reynolds General Store, with two large windows full of things, the door between them. Men were loafing, whittling, talking and spitting along the high board walk. There were small stores, The Bank of Mansfield, a Boston Racket Store with "Opera House" painted on the windows upstairs, Hoover's Livery Stable and horses in a feed lot, then another big house inside a wire fence. Past a blacksmith shop the dusty road went downhill to cross a little bridge. The long hillside was orchard and pasture, but houses began where the road went up again beyond the bridge. In all there must have been a dozen houses, in fenced yards with gates, behind paths through the weeds on both sides of the road.

All the houses had front porches; all were painted and trimmed with different colors and wooden lace. Behind them were vegetable gardens and clotheslines, barns and chicken houses; some had pigpens. Two had an upstairs; one of these had a bay window and a cupola. Behind the houses on our right was the railroad enbankment; behind those on the left, two more houses and a high grassy hill against the sky.

At the top of the road's long climb stood the schoolhouse where I would go to school. It stood square, two stories high, with windows all around, and its bell tower up above the double doors. All beyond it was woods; it was in the edge of the woods but not a single stump remained on the ground trodden bare and hard about it. There was a well beside it; behind it a woodshed and two privies: Boys and Girls.

I looked as long as I could, but the road turned away from the schoolhouse to follow the railroad track. The wheel tracks went beside the iron rails with the row of poles holding a telegraph wire on glass knobs above them. There were two houses in the woods; then the road turned into the woods and left the railroad behind us.

Now there was nothing but woods on either side, and the two wheel tracks went straight and slowly downward. Between them were stumps and big rocks. The wagon jolted and lurched over rocks in the dust and the horses' iron shoes clattered on them.

From the talk over my head I learned how lucky it was that the last cent had been just enough to pay for the salt pork and cornmeal. We could make out all right now, selling wood, and do well when the apple trees were in bearing. Paying off the mortgage would be easy then. Three hundred dollars at twelve percent, pounded every three months. (Why would they be pounded? I wondered.) My mother could do the arithmetic in her head. They ought to be able to carry it if they kept their health.

Either then or later I learned from such talk that some very foolish man had bought all those little apple trees from a smart salesman though he had no cleared land. When they came in their bundles, he had no clearing to set them out in; but he had signed papers, so he had to mortgage the land to pay for them. Then he just gave up. Between two days, he left the land and the cabin, the little apple trees root-buried in a trench, and the mortgage. So my father and mother got them from the banker.

The road went up again, it seemed to go almost vertically up a long, long hill, but my father turned the horses away from it, onto a fainter track in a valley. Beside us now a stream of water as clear as glass ran over flat ledges and through shallow pools. In a little while the wagon tracks turned to ford a pool. The horses stopped to drink and my mother said, "Here we are!" She asked me what I thought of it, but I saw nothing to think about. The creek came from our own spring, she told me. Across the creek the woods went up a low hill in the yellow light of the sinking sun; the wheel tracks went on down the curve of the creek and trees hid them.

My father drove up the hill through the woods. The horses climbed clumsily, the flat rocks slipping under their feet. At the top of the hill we came into a tiny clearing at the edge of a deep ravine, and there stood a little log house.

Quick as a squirrel, I was down over the wheel and around the corner of logs' ends. A rough, thick door stood open; I was in the house, I was in a narrow little room, its floor of earth and dead leaves, but beyond a doorway was a larger room that had a wooden floor. This room was bare and clean, it smelled like the woods, dead leaves were blown into its corners. There was a big fireplace and sure enough, as that woman had said, no windows. There was a square hole in the wall of peeled logs; an empty hole, but it had a rough wooden door hanging open, like the house door.

Nothing more was to be seen there. But I hadn't noticed that in the narrow room the logs of the wall around the door were papered with newspapers. Large black letters in curley-cues stopped me; I stood and read: "Carter's Little Liver Pills," and a philosophical question which I kept try-

Rocky Ridge Farm in Mansfield after Almanzo had cleared a good deal of the land. Laura probably took this photograph about 1910.

The cabin we lived in during the first winter in Mansfield. It was part of the barn when this picture was taken. The horses are the team which brought us down from Dakota. My father is sitting in a buggy for which he traded the hack, when we were rich enough to have a wagon AND a buggy.

ing and failing to answer for so long afterward that I have never forgotten it: What is life without a liver?

That problem was too much for me; for the moment, I postponed the struggle with it. Outside, some chunks of bark had fallen from the house wall, and between all the logs was yellow clay, dry and hard and cracked to bits. Not far away the path from the door went down, steeper than stairs, into the ravine. As usual, my mother called to me to be careful.

The ravine was shadowy, darker in its narrow bottom. It ended in one huge rock as big as a big house. Behind the rock was a hollow sound of running water, and water ran from beneath it into a little pool as round as a washtub and half as deep. Ferns hung over the darling pool, and from a bough above it dangled a hollowed-out gourd for dipping up the water.

I drank a delicious cold gourdful, looking up and up the mountainside above the spring. It was all dark woods, only the very tips of the highest trees in sudden yellow light. All down the dark ravine the water chuckled eerily. Something moved stealthily in the leaves under the bushes. I clambered up the path as fast as I could.

The horses were unhitched and picketed, the hens in their coop on the ground. My father and mother were taking out things over the wagon's opened end-gate. We would eat supper outdoors and sleep one more night in the wagon. My mother meant to scrub that cabin floor from top to bottom

A neighbor's cabin.   My father is pictured by it in his "buffalo coat," which was made from the skin of a buffalo killed in Dakota.

before we moved into it. We could still see well enough in the shadowy daylight but inside the wagon it was too dark to find things. My father rummaged for the lantern.

He pressed the spring that lifted its thick glass globe, he touched the match-flame to the wick and carefully lowered the globe into its place, and suddenly the lantern was shining in darkness. He held it up, looking for a place to hang it, and there in the edge of its light stood a strange man.

The man's feet were bare, his pants were patched over patches and torn. He was tall, thin, bony, and his eyes glittered from a bush of hair and whiskers. He came a step nearer and quick as a snake my mother's hand slid into the pocket where her revolver was. She waited, ready. Slowly my father said, "Hello there."

The man said he wanted work, he was looking for a chance to work for something to eat. My father answered that we were just moving in, as he could see; we didn't have work to give anybody. Too bad, but maybe better luck in town, just over the next hill, not much more than a mile to the west.

"You got a good place here," the man said. He was bony, but big. After a minute my father said it would be a good place someday, he guessed. Then we all stood silent as if we couldn't move.

The man began to talk quietly, slowly, almost dreamily. They had to get something to eat, he said. His wife and five children were down in the wagon by the creek. They had been traveling all summer looking for work. They could not go on any longer. This was the third day they'd had nothing to eat. He had to get work, so he came up the wagon tracks— They couldn't go on without something to eat.

He stopped, there was nothing more to say. Nothing to do. Now I knew what happened when you had nothing to eat. What happens is, nothing.

Suddenly, my father was talking and moving quickly, not deliberate at all. He said he needed help making wood, provided the man would come help him tomorrow, he'd divide what little— He was reaching into the wagon. At sight of the slab of salted fat pork my mother cried out, "Manly, *no! We've got Rose.*" He paid no attention. The butcher knife in his hand cut through the white meat. He opened a corner of the sack and poured cornmeal into the little tin pail. He was asking, did the man have a good ax? He said they'd start early, at sun-up, put in a good day's work and if the wood sold he'd treat the man right. Bring an ax if he had one. Be sure to bring back the pail. That's all right, don't mention it, see you tomorrow.

The man was gone into the darkness. He had not said a word. Afterward my mother always said that she expected never to see that vagabond again, nor her tin pail, either. At the time she said nothing. My father made the fire under the camp stove and she cooked supper. We had fried salt pork and corn-dodgers, and slept in the wagon.

The man woke us in the false dawn, bringing the tin pail and his ax. He was a better woodsman than my father. All that day while my mother and I cleaned the house and lugged things from the wagon to put on the dry, scrubbed floor, they worked in the woods. They worked as long as they could see. Then my mother held the lantern and they took the top and curtains off the wagon, and stacked up high in it all the stove wood that it would hold.

Early next morning my father set out to sell the wood in town. The man worked with a will while he was gone. He was gone all day. At night he had not come. The strange man went down the hill, my mother lighted the lamp, turned low to save the kerosene. Still it was some time before we heard the wagon jolting. My mother lighted the lantern, then said I'd better take it to him.

I rushed out with it. The wagon box was empty and I almost shouted, "You sold it!"

"Finally I did," my father said in triumph.

"How much did you get for it?" I asked. He was beginning to unharness the horses. He bragged, "Fifty cents."

I set down the lantern and ran into the house to tell my mother, "Fifty cents! He sold it all for fifty cents!" Her whole face trembled and seemed to melt into softness, she sighed a long sigh. "Aren't you glad?" I exulted.

"Glad? Of course I'm glad!" she snapped at me and to herself, "Oh, thanks be!"

I ran out again, I pranced out, to tell my father how glad

she was. And he said, with a sound of crying in his voice, "Oh, why did you tell her? I wanted to surprise her."

You do such things, little things, horrible, cruel, without thinking, not meaning to. You have done it; nothing can undo it. This is a thing you can never forget.

How long that man worked with my father I don't remember. I cannot remember his name nor anything at all about his family camping down by the creek. Surely I knew those children; they must have been there for weeks. I remember that he and my father were roofing the little log barn, the day I chased the rabbit.

The leaves had fallen from all the trees but the oaks then, and the oaks wore their winter red that day. There was light snow or frost underfoot, so cold that it burned my bare feet, and my breath puffed white in the air. I chased that rabbit over the hills, up and down and back again until, exhausted, it hid in a hollow log; I stopped up the log's ends with rocks and fetched both men from their work on the roof to chop out the rabbit and kill it.

The day was Saturday; I was going to school then. For Sunday dinner we had rabbit stew, with gravy on mashed potatoes and on our cornbread. And on Monday I found in my lunch-pail at school one of that rabbit's legs; my mother had saved it and packed it with the cornbread in the little tin pail, to surprise me.

The man and his family must have gone on west or south, early that winter. He must have earned provisions for the trip. I remember walking to school through the snowy woods in my shoes and stockings, hearing the thuds of my father's ax sounding fainter as I went; and coming home with the sunset red behind me to hear the whirr-whirr of the crosscut saw growing sharper in the frosty air. The ax was too heavy for my mother; my father would not trust her with its sharpness, but she could safely handle one end of the crosscut saw.

Winter evenings were cozy in the cabin. The horses were warm in the little barn, the hens in the new wooden coop. Snow banked against the log walls and long icicles hung from the eaves. A good fire of hickory logs burned in the fireplace. In its heat, over a newspaper spread on the hearth, my father worked oil into the harness-straps between his oily-black hands. I sat on the floor, carefully building a house of corncobs, and my mother sat by the table, knitting needles flashing while she knitted warm woolen socks for my father and read to us from a book propped under the kerosene lamp. She read us Tennyson's poems and Scott's poems; those books were ours. And she read us Prescott's *Conquest of Mexico*, and *Conquest of Peru*, and *The Green Mountain Boys*, and *John Halifax, Gentleman*. She read us *The Leatherstocking Tales*, and another true book, the biggest of all: *Ancient, Medieval and Modern History*. I borrowed those from the shelf of lending-books in the Fourth Reader room at school. The teachers let me borrow them, though I wasn't in Fourth Reader yet.

I remember the Sunday afternoon when my father and mother planned the new house. We had got the cow that spring; I must have been ten years old, going on eleven. On Sunday afternoons in warm weather, when company wasn't spending the day with us or we were not spending it in town with the Cooleys, my father and mother in their Sunday clothes went walking sedately over the land while I, in mine, minded the cabin. They had cleared twenty acres and set out all the little apple trees, and we had the cow, that Sunday afternoon when they decided where to build the house.

From my swing in the oak tree by the cabin, Fido and I saw them standing and talking under the huge old white-oak tree not far away. They talked a long while. Then my father went to lead the cow to water and change her picket-peg, and my mother called me to see the spot where our house would be.

It would be under the great old white-oak at the edge of the hill where we stood. Here the ground sloped more gently down into the ravine and rose steeply up the wooded mountain to the south. You could see the brook running from the widening mouth of the ravine and curving to the north and east around the base of the rounded hill. You could hear the water rippling over the limestone ledges. It was springtime; the hickory trees on the hill were in young green leaves, the oak leaves were pink, and all the flinty ground beneath them was covered with one blue-purple mat of dog's-tooth violets. Along the brook the sarvice trees were blooming misty white. The ancient white-oak was lively with dozens of young squirrels whisking into and out of their nests in the hollow branches.

My mother stood under it in her brown-sprigged white lawn dress, her long braid hanging down her back. Below the curled bangs her eyes were as purple-blue as the violets. It would be a white house, she said, all built from our farm. Everything we needed to build it was on the land: good oak beams and boards, stones for the foundation and the fireplace. The house would have large windows looking west across the brook, over the gentle little valley and up the wooded hills that hid the town, to the sunset colors in the sky. There would be a nice big porch to the north, cool on hot summer afternoons. The kitchen would be big enough to hold a wood stove for winter and one of the new kerosene stoves that wouldn't heat up the place worse in summer. Every window would be screened with mosquito netting. There would be a well, with a pump, just outside the kitchen door; no more lugging water from the spring. And in the parlor there would be a bookcase, no, *two* bookcases, big bookcases full of books, and a hanging lamp to read them by, in winter evenings by the fireplace.

When the mortgage is paid, in only a few more years, she said, and when the orchard is in bearing, if prices are good then, we will fence the whole place with wire and build the

Part of Rocky Ridge

Farm as it looks today.

Laura's dream realized: the house that she and Almanzo built of materials from the farm. The wellhouse is outside the kitchen door. The fence was added after her death in 1957; she wouldn't allow one built. The home is now preserved as a memorial museum by the Laura Ingalls Wilder Home Association of Mansfield, Missouri.

barn bigger; we will have more stock by then. And after that, we can begin to build the house.

She woke from the dream with a start and a Goodness! it's chore-time! I'd better take the milk pail to my father, she said, and feed the hens before they went to roost; don't forget to fill their water-pans, and bring in the eggs; be careful not to break one. Oh, now that we had the cow, we'd have a treat for Sunday supper, French toast with that wild honey, to surprise my father. How wonderful it was to have a cow again.

While I scattered corn for the hens, fetched water from the spring to fill their pans, and hunted for eggs that the broody hens hid in the haymow, in the straw stack, and even in the wild grasses, I heard her whistling in the cabin, getting supper.

Format by Jean Krulis
Set in Linotype Janson
Printed by the Murray Printing Co.
HARPER & ROW, PUBLISHERS, INCORPORATED

B
921
Wil   Wilder, Laura Ingalls
       On the Way Home

c.2

DATE DUE

NOV 30 '89		APR. 06 1995	16
JAN 2 2 1992			
FEB. 1 7 1993			
MAR 25 1993			
OCT. 0 5 1993			
OCT. 2 1 1993			
NOV. 1 6 1993			
MAR 0 3 1994			
MAY 1 7 1994			
JAN 2 6 1995			
FEB 0 9 1995			
FEB 0 9 1995			

9-149